SOMETHING BETTER

SOMETHING BETTER

7 Principles to Get the Best out of Life

By Dr. Cassie J Williams

Printed in the United States of America

First Edition

ISBN: 979-8-9985185-2-2

Editing and Interior layout by
Cindy L. Hyde
Hyde Virtual Agency

Dedication

I dedicate this book to everyone who deserves and wants Something Better out of life.

In Memory

I thank God for allowing my mother, Jannie Johnson Jones, to show me the value of hard work, determination, perseverance, and generosity. You graced the statement, “It won’t be like this always.” Those words of wisdom have given me hope in the toughest of circumstances.

I am grateful that you taught me important lessons, such as how to grow a garden and how to make the most of what you have in your pantry when there's more month than money.

With few resources, you raised four children. With only a GED, you instilled in us the importance of education, reading, and, most of all, faith in God to carry us through. The example you set gave me a thirst for ‘Something Better’. I will love you forever. I carry you in my spirit.

Though I didn't grow up with him, I cherish the adult memories I had with my dad, Preston Jones, Sr. The outings to Atkinson Candy Kitchen, Golden Corral (his favorite place to eat because there was no waiting), and the laughter we shared is priceless. I learned to forgive even the deepest pain suppressed by anger and hurt. I am grateful that we shared the love of family history and the hunger to know more about them.

I am blessed to have had you in my life. I love you. You are my dad.

To my sister Deidre, I miss you. You were the smartest of us all. You got the highest grades in school, and I tried my best to emulate you. Your cooking was superb, and without a doubt could have been an entrée on a restaurant's menu. You endured some tough times, but your fight spoke volumes to those who knew you best. I cherish our sister circle always.

Acknowledgements

I want to thank God, Who is the Creator of life. He gave me the vision of 'Something Better' over fifteen years ago, and now it is here. I love Him with all my heart. I thank Him for placing people in my circle to encourage me, support me, and tell me the truth in love.

You are an AWESOME God!

To my husband, Darell, this journey has not been easy, but we have endured and still run our race with the good fight of faith. Thank you for your encouragement and prayers. I love you.

To our children and grandchildren, I love you to life. Thank you for your support, laughs, and desire to live a life of purpose.

Thank you to all my friends and the sister circle of love. You have all encouraged, prayed, and supported me, and allowed me to become a snippet in your lives. I am so proud of all of you for what you have accomplished and the 'Something Better' to come.

Foreword

Some connections are God-ordained. They happen at just the right time and spark something bigger than either person expected. That's exactly how I would describe meeting Dr. Cassie J. Williams.

As an ordained minister, life coach, and faith-based counselor, I've had the blessing of walking with many people in search of healing, purpose, and truth. But Cassie isn't just another voice in the crowd. She's a force—spirit-led, deeply compassionate, and bold enough to say what many are still afraid to admit.

We connected through our shared calling: helping others find spiritual healing, emotional restoration, and practical hope. Through ministering the Word, prayer, life coaching, and counseling, we've stood in the trenches with people, sometimes broken, often weary, but always seeking something better. That phrase became more than a passing conversation. It became Cassie's message. And now, it's this book.

Something Better isn't just a title. It's a testimony. It's the heartbeat of a woman who's faced storms and still chooses to rise with grace. Cassie has poured her story, her faith, and her wisdom onto these pages with honesty and depth.

You'll feel it as you read. She doesn't sugarcoat the pain, and she doesn't preach from a pedestal. She writes from the valley and the mountaintop—both places she's walked through.

I've had the honor of standing beside her in ministry and supporting the creative process behind this book. And I can say with complete confidence—these words are real. They've been prayed over, wrestled through, and written with you in mind.

If you've ever asked, "Is this all there is?" this book is for you. If you've dared to hope that healing is possible, that life could be fuller, and that God still shows up, Cassie's voice will echo that truth in your spirit.

She's not just qualified to write this book because of her credentials. She's qualified because she's lived it. And now she's handing you a roadmap to do the same.

Get ready.

Your *Something Better* starts now.

With grace and purpose,
Rev. Cindy Hyde
Ordained Minister | Professional Life Coach
www.cindylhyde.com

Table of Contents

Introduction

We live in a world with endless possibilities, yet only a minute few seem to have access. Such limits may lead one to conclude that God created some people to be successful and get the best that life offers, while others cannot get past the struggle. I refute that belief.

The Creator is a just and loving God. He cannot do such things. That is not in His character. He says,

I (God) wish above all things that you prosper and be in health, even as your soul prospers."
3 John 2 (NIV)

Furthermore, Hebrews 11:40 (NIV) states,

"Since God had planned something better for us so that only together with us would they be made perfect."

The fact that you were not born into a wealthy family does not mean you cannot be prosperous, receive something better, live better, or be better.

What is wealth?

The viewpoint determines the interpretation.

I have been with people whose parents or grandparents were wealthy, yet they wished they were average. "At least my parents would have spent more time with me," some would say. In adulthood, they longed for quality time. Time could be their wealth. In Isaiah 43:19 (NIV), God still promised us, saying,

"See, I am doing a new thing! Now it springs up; do you not perceive it? I am making a way in the wilderness and streams in the wasteland."

Everyone starts life without complete knowledge or possessions. When a baby is born, do they already know how to walk? Was the child born holding dollars or gold in his hands? Of truth, life is an arena of choices. We are products of our parents' choices.

Our lives are products of our choices. What and who we know influences our choices in most cases. "Knowledge is power," is a common saying. The difference between you and what you desire is "What you do not know."

Your desires would have been met if you knew what they were and how to get them. So, our choices, the steps we take, and the faith we hold, anchor success and the best of life.

We live in a world where external achievements and material possessions often measure success and happiness. Yet, despite attaining these markers, one may feel a lingering sense of dissatisfaction. Our lives are a whirlwind of activity, but we yearn for deeper fulfillment and a sense of purpose.

If success were all about material things, why does depression linger among the wealthy?

Why does one go from relationship to relationship?

Getting the best out of life takes more than chasing success. It calls for vision, discipline, and a deeper sense of purpose. This book is not about abandoning ambition but aligning passion with principles that bring lasting joy and satisfaction.

Now, imagine standing at a crossroads where one path leads to a life of mere existence and the other to a life of extraordinary fulfillment. What if the secret to unlocking a richer, more meaningful life lay not in grand gestures but in seven transformative principles?

This book shares seven powerful principles. If you can learn these principles and put them into practice, you will soon look back and not recognize yourself in the rearview mirror. It is a journey to revolutionize how you live, think, and aspire. It is based on common sense and coaching analysis over the past twenty years. If you doubt now, it's okay. But read to the end and test your creative ability to change.

Chapter 1

A Change of Mindset

Have you ever wondered why certain people seem to go through complex life challenges, yet they come out stronger each time? Do they always look different from what they have passed through? Why do others seem stuck in a cycle of frustration, poverty, and mediocrity despite their efforts? Is the secret to success and getting the best out of life not in the circumstances one passes through but in one's mindset?

Well, there is no need to guess; it is true. Your mindset will usually determine your outcome. The surrounding things are determined by what is within you. The wisest man that ever lived said,

"As a man thinks in his heart, so he is."
Proverbs 23:7 (NIV)

He did not say, "So he will be"; he said, "So he is." So, it is a present reality.

Your persona can become your reality. By this alone, you can set the tone of your present and future. Amid challenges, when you picture yourself winning the battle, you are what you are thinking and not what you are experiencing.

The journey to achieving the best in life begins with a strategic shift in how you think, focusing on more positive thoughts. It involves believing you deserve and will receive the best, no matter the circumstances.

I am at a loss for words when people think or expect the worst in every situation. How can one say they will fail an exam before taking it? Or when someone says, "I know I'm not going to get this job. I'm just going for this job interview; let it not be as if I didn't try." They justify negativity by claiming realism or self-protection from previous pain.

Realistic? What is realistic about negativity, or do you want negativity to come to pass in your life? Negativity should not be familiar in one's life. In other words, you should not become so accustomed to negativity that it dominates you, preventing you from achieving prosperity.

Embrace the positive. Words spoken about your life, over your life, and situations are confessions that hold enormous power. When someone feeds you something negative, for instance, "You won't ever make it" or "You're useless," it does not mean you have to take the plate. Cancel those negative words spoken over you. And please, do not conform and profess negativity over yourself.

If only you knew the power your tongue and words possess. You would use them to your advantage. No matter how fearful you are, speaking negatively about yourself should never cross your mind.

"Life and death are in the power of the tongue, and those who love it will eat its fruits."
Proverbs 8:21 (NIV)

Did you get that? Life and death? Power? Life is breathing, moving, growing, being, living, and having purpose. Death is the opposite. Death means no life, dormant, undoing, a permanent end.

Power means authority, ability, or influence. You have that power in what you say. You can speak into your life and get a different outcome than where you began.

The Power of Perspective

Think about two people facing the same challenge. One sees the reach as unattainable and thinks it came to destroy him. The other sees it as a stepping stone, an opportunity for growth, experience, and strength. Which one will end with a greater reward? The difference between the two lies in what one has experienced and one's internal perspective.

Those who believe life is about luck live by chance instead of embracing change. They focus on their downfalls rather than trusting in the divine. In contrast, those who view life through the lens of responsibility understand that success requires intention.

They remain focused, disciplined, and committed. Though struggles may arise, they persevere—not because the path is easy. But because they are determined to see the process through and produce something meaningful.

Our mindset acts as a lens through which we interpret and relate to the environment and the world. A growth-oriented mindset can convert challenges into stepping stones. The opposite is true; a negative, fixed, small mindset can turn even the most minute challenge into a significant roadblock.

The first step to getting the best out of life is intentionally changing your perspective on one thing at a time. Stay focused. Train your mind to see every situation as a chance to learn and improve.

Life does not give you what you deserve, but what you permit. If you consistently allow negative, toxic things and people to infiltrate your life, you are bound to spiral down. It is time to shift your perspective. Start in your mind, then in your voice.

Your voice! Your power!

To get the best out of life, you must learn to speak healing words to yourself. No matter how down you feel or the challenges that come your way on the journey, never speak negative words about your life. Instead, confess positivity and speak words that are healthy for your soul.

God, our Creator, answers not only your prayers, but also the thoughts of your heart. Ephesians 3:20 notes that God can do much more than you can imagine or think.

What is your imagination casting?

Something big or small?

Believe you deserve better, no matter how big or small. God said to test Him. He is faithful to His word.

A victor's mindset may be rigid for some people, but it is not unattainable. Do not normalize what is keeping you at a disadvantage; be it your race, nationality, gender, education, living environment, or the fact that you were never on the equal playing field from the beginning.

See it. Acknowledge it. Take steps to move to something better.

Whether you are zealous, optimistic, tenacious, a go-getter, or a don't-take-no-for-an-answer type of person, it stems from your mindset. Suppose you are a laid-back, pessimistic, expecting-the-worst kind of person. In either case, the outcome will meet your expectations. Again, life will not give you what you deserve, but what you permit.

Sometimes, people do not have negative mindsets because they want to. It may be because of a backlog of negative experiences that makes one expect the worst. This could be a coping mechanism that needs further evaluation through counseling, coaching, or other therapy.

Nonetheless, wage war against negative voices in your mind telling you that you are not good enough, can never make it in life, and do not deserve something better. It is a lie of the enemy to keep people bound and imprisoned in their minds.

Lizzy, the mother of twelve-year-old Luke, continuously talked negatively about her son. Her words are not worth repeating. We saw each other in a shopping center one afternoon. The conversation began with a warm greeting and a catch-up on the last couple of weeks. No sooner had our conversation begun, she started talking negatively about her son.

I stopped her before she could get the next sentence out. I firmly, yet lovingly said, "Don't be disappointed if your son turns out to be just what you speak of him."

I continued, "I hope he doesn't live up to those *words of affirmation*." Perhaps her words were replayed in the son's mind to the point of hopelessness, which was carried out in his behavior.

Lizzy concluded our meet and greet, stating she had other errands to run. I know she may not have liked what I said, but I believe she will think about my words the next time she speaks of her son's character.

Words have the power to build or tear down. It takes courage to begin changing your mindset. But you can have a victor's mindset or a victim's mindset. The choice is always yours. Speak new, positive words to drown out the old voices that have taken hold in your mind. You can do this. Allow yourself to believe it.

Chapter One Questions

A Change of Mind

1. Formed habits are not easily broken, so changing your mindset will take work. Identify one habit you are willing to change that could have a significant impact on your life.

2. Massive change requires small steps. What small steps, repeated daily, can you implement today to help you achieve your goals?

3. The voice in your head may narrate negative thoughts. Ignite a change of perspective by affirming yourself. List 3 positive affirmations about yourself (you may seek help from family/friends).

Chapter 2

Connected to God

Everything about you connects to God. Your life, your being, your future, your destiny, everything! It is not about being a Christian or not being a Christian. It is about Who created you.

Similarly, car manufacturers detail the unique qualities and specifications of their cars. That is the same way God, your maker, knows all the tiny details of your life. He knows all the qualities you possess that make you unique.

"Before I formed you in the womb, I knew you before you were born, I set you apart..."
Jeremiah 1:5 (NIV)

"But God even knows how many hairs you have on your head. Don't be afraid. You are worth much more than many sparrows."
Luke 12:7(NCV)

He knows all your talents, strengths, weaknesses, and more about you than you know about yourself. God, knowing all things, is your best guide. You have a role to play in God's big picture. One of the most tragic things that can happen to someone is to live year after year on this Earth and not realize that they have a purpose. A purpose that stretches far beyond their current circumstance.

We cannot live how we want without sacrifice. It is either a sacrifice for God or a sacrifice for the world. Why is this? It is because, as humans, our mind's eye is limited. Remember, we do not know the end from the beginning; only God does. One can only guess but cannot confidently say what will happen tomorrow.

Only God, the Omniscient one, the only wise God who knows tomorrow, knows for sure what will happen each day before the day begins. For this reason, you should maximize your time on Earth and obtain the best out of life as you connect to the Source - God.

Remember, He numbered every hair on your head? God is intentional about us. Why else would He have numbered the hairs on our heads?

That means if we lose a strand of hair, God knows it. If He keeps track of seemingly unimportant things, how much more do you do with your life? God is much more interested in your life and future than you think. He wants what is best for you more than you want what is best for your life.

Is it not interesting to know that King Solomon, the wealthiest and wisest man, was godly and reverenced God? Findings indicate that King Solomon's wealth is estimated at $2.1 trillion in today's currency. King Solomon had accumulated a vast amount of gold and silver, with silver becoming as common in Jerusalem as stone.

Solomon's wealth was more substantial than the combined wealth of the top five wealthiest men. It is more important to know that he understood the place of God in his life. His outstanding success stemmed from God. God gave him all he had because the level of sacrifice demonstrated his love and service to Him, which he offered to God. He said,

"You can make many plans, but the Lord's purpose will prevail."
Proverbs 19:21 (NIV)

There is no better wisdom than knowing that you cannot get life's best without God. You can acquire many things, but there will still be an emptiness that material things cannot fill. Only God can fill that void. Material things are temporal. God's plan has a beautiful life destined for you. Faith in God's plan for your prosperity diminishes the need for personal striving.

When you understand your role in God's agenda, you will not see the need to envy or compete with anyone. You can be happy for them, clap for them, encourage and wish them well, but you will never envy them.

The reason is that everybody's purpose in life is unique, and nobody's purpose is superior. God designed it so that we will all have unique contributions to make, and each of our contributions complements each other.

If you take a fish out of the water and place it on a high slope to see if it can learn to fly like an eagle, you would be left with no fish in no time because the fish would die.

Trying to help the fish ultimately led to its destruction. Fish are not designed to fly like the eagle; in the same way, the eagle is not intended to swim underwater. This does not make the fish better than the eagle or vice versa; it is diverse in purpose.

Take note: the day you step outside the purpose of God for your life is the day you start wandering in the desert. Our purpose is the core of our lives, the reason we are here on Earth, and what gives us the strength to face each day. Just like fish, we cannot be fulfilled when we leave our natural habitat.

Your purpose might not keep you at the forefront. You may be thinking, "Do people see this thing I am doing? Is it affecting anyone's life in the least?" When we watch movies, we only see the main characters on the screen.

Still, for the main characters to be on the screen, there is an entire production crew behind the scenes whose input is equally crucial in making that movie.

Your purpose does not put you on the stage for people to clap for you. If you get applause, that is great, but that does not determine the outcome of your purpose. Neither does it mean you should relent in your efforts. Your unique input is needed. Whatever you do, do it diligently, and God will reward you. Until you live for something bigger than yourself, getting the best out of life will be a mirage.

Discover Your Purpose

To live a fulfilled life, connecting to God is paramount to your purpose. God knew our purpose before we were born. It remains for us to ask Him what He created us for. We do that through communication with Him (Prayer).

When you discover your purpose, life becomes easier because you are no longer chasing meaningless things. Still, you are working according to what is written about you. I am not talking about what people say about you or the negative comments on social media. You can write your script with the Creator's hand guiding you.

Everyone's Role in Life is Different.

Circumstances and tragedies may come, but your responsibility remains—to live fully in the purpose God placed within you. A life outside of purpose isn't just misdirected; it's unfulfilled. Imagine if God called you to influence nations as a leader in government, yet you chose a different path—perhaps as a teacher or doctor.

While you might still make a difference, you'd be operating beneath your divine capacity. Purpose isn't just about doing good—it's about doing what you were *created* to do. Anything less is a partial version of the life God intended for you.

Understand that when you are in line with God's purpose for your life, God will give you everything you need to fulfill it. It will not all come at once but remember that one's life is not lived in a day. God will give you what you need when you need it. No sooner, no later. When you focus on your vision, God will provide everything you need on the journey to your purpose.

How to Discover Your Purpose

When you see someone with a syringe, what comes to your mind as the person's title? Would you call them a lawyer or a doctor? When you see someone with a hammer, nails, and some wood, will you call him a chef or a carpenter?

Just like certain tools reveal a person's profession, the gifts God placed within us reveal our purpose. When God created you, He equipped you with specific tools—your talents, passions, and abilities—designed for your unique assignment. Want to know what you were made to do?

Look at the tools in your hands. Your gifts aren't random; they are clues pointing directly to your calling. Discovering your purpose begins with recognizing what God has already placed within you. In his book *Purpose Driven Life*, Rick Warren talked about SHAPE and defined it as:

S – Spiritual gifts
H – Heart
A – Abilities
P – Personality
E – Experiences

When you ask God why He created you, also examine your SHAPE. No two humans on Earth can have the same SHAPE. It is worth noting that God does not waste resources or do anything without intention. So, whatever you find in yourself and your life, God put it there for a purpose. Remember, you are "fearfully and wonderfully made." Psalm 139:14 (NIV).

Everything you have or will experience is designed to make you better. All is not wasted. Once it comes into full manifestation, you can see why some things happened the way they did. Let’s review your uniqueness through the lens of each of the Spiritual gifts.

Spiritual gifts

The Bible outlines a variety of spiritual gifts, each given by God to equip believers to serve, build up others, and fulfill His purposes. These gifts are generally grouped into two main categories: manifestation gifts and ministry gifts.

The manifestation gifts are listed in 1 Corinthians 12:8–10 and include the following: Word of Wisdom, Word of Knowledge, Faith, Gifts of Healing, Working of Miracles, Prophecy, Discerning of Spirits, Speaking in Different Kinds of Tongues, and Interpretation of Tongues. These are supernatural abilities given by the Holy Spirit as He wills and are used to reveal God's power and presence in real time.

The ministry gifts, sometimes referred to as motivational or leadership gifts, are mentioned in Romans chapter 12 and Ephesians chapter 4. These include the gifts of Teaching, Giving, Encouragement (Exhortation), Leadership, Mercy, Hospitality, Evangelism, Apostleship, Shepherding (Pastoring), and Administration. These gifts often shape how a person serves others over the long term and reflect the personality and calling God placed within them.

Whether operating in spiritual power or practical service, these gifts are not random. They are intentional, divinely appointed tools to help you walk in your God-given purpose.

Heart

Your heart represents your inner desires, passions, dreams, values, and burdens—the things that move you deeply and give your life meaning.

What are you naturally drawn to?

What issues stir your compassion or ignite your righteous anger?

These aren't random emotions or preferences. They are spiritual clues placed in you by God to point you toward your purpose. Your heart reveals what you care about most, what brings you joy, and what breaks your heart. Whether it's a passion for mentoring youth, writing stories, defending justice, or comforting the broken, what captures your heart is often a reflection of your divine assignment.

Abilities

Everyone has God-given abilities, whether they seem natural or learned. These are the skills and talents you excel at, often with ease or joy. They may not seem spiritual on the surface, but they are part of how God equips you for your purpose.

Singing, solving problems, writing, managing money, organizing, cooking, encouraging others, painting, public speaking, and thinking critically are all examples of abilities that can be used to serve God and others.

Your abilities may be evident in your work, at home, or in your community. You may be the one who always finds solutions, keeps things running, brings peace, or creates beauty where others see none.

No ability is insignificant.

What you do well can be a key to where God is leading you. When surrendered to Him, even the simplest skill becomes powerful in His hands.

Personality

Your personality encompasses your natural temperament—whether you're introverted or extroverted, structured or spontaneous, reserved or expressive, cautious or adventurous, a quiet thinker or an outspoken visionary. These unique traits influence how you process experiences, form relationships, and navigate challenges. They shape the lens through which you see the world and help define how you express your values, passions, and calling. Your personality is not just a reflection of who you are, but also a guide in how you are meant to impact the lives of others.

Experiences

Every season of your life, whether joyful or painful, has shaped who you are today. Your background, family upbringing, education, work history, traumas, triumphs, and even failures all carry meaning. God does not waste anything you have been through.

The things you have endured, overcome, or struggled with often point directly to the people you are called to help. Whether it's surviving abuse, growing up in poverty, overcoming addiction, raising children, grieving loss, or rebuilding after brokenness, your experiences become part of your ministry.

They are proof of God's faithfulness and the very tools He uses to reach others through your life. Your story, with all its highs and lows, is not just yours to carry. It is part of your calling.

Together, your spiritual gifts, heart, abilities, personality, and life experiences point clearly toward your God-given purpose. Someone with the gifts of teaching, wisdom, and compassion may feel called to mentor youth. A natural encourager who has overcome grief may walk with others through loss.

A skilled organizer who has experienced chaos may help families find peace and structure. A person who once struggled with addiction might now lead others to recovery. No matter what you've walked through or what strengths you carry, God weaves it all into something meaningful and impactful.

Pursue Your Passion

Our purpose and passion align to fulfill our why. If your passion is singing, consider taking singing lessons, attending rehearsals, and practicing regularly to enhance your skills. When one recognizes one's passion, one must move toward cultivating it from the inside out. Making that passion rise to the peak takes work and connection with people.

Remember, it only takes one person's investment in you that can catapult you into victory. Jethro invested in Moses (Exodus 2). Mordecai invested in Esther. (Esther 4).

Who has invested in you, whether short or long-term, that has helped you in your current moment?

The investment may come in a season or can be throughout your lifetime.

Inspiration from God: The Blessing of a Third Eye

A fashion designer once said her inspiration for her beautiful fashion pieces comes from the Holy Spirit. She said that she envisioned designs she had not seen before in her dreams. She would wake up, immediately go to her design desk, and begin working.

I was watching a YouTube clip of Steve Harvey from the *Woman Thou Art Loosed* Conference. He talked about seeing things that others could not see. He described it as being the "third eye." This "third eye" allowed him to see the comedy in things others could not see. The gift has allowed him to travel the world, giving others a moment to decompress from their cares and embrace laughter, which is good for the soul.

Many people may share similar gifts or callings, but what sets you apart is your unique story, your lived experiences, and the skills you've cultivated along the way. Above all, it’s the God factor—His presence in your life that gives you a divine advantage. When God is with you, you don’t just participate; you stand out. His favor, guidance, and power make the ordinary extraordinary and turn your calling into a testimony.

God can help you get to 'something better.' It is not enough to depend on your knowledge and skills; you need inspiration from God. To get the most out of life, you need to see what others are not seeing.

Chapter Two Questions

Connected to God

1. What spiritual aspects can you lean on for strength and assurance?

2. Purpose is powerful. What gives your life its meaning?

3. What did your 15-year-old self-imagine you would be doing right now?

4. What kind of person do you want to be in 5 years? What sacrifices are you willing to make to get there?

5. Over the last 6 months, when have you felt the most alive and living purposefully?

6. If you could start your career over, what would you do differently? Why?

Chapter 3

1st Principle–Defining Target

Goal setting is developing an action plan to motivate and guide a person toward a goal. Having goals for things we want to do and working towards them is essential for living without regret. It gives us a sense of meaning and purpose and points us in the direction we want to go.

Setting goals is vital to success. I encourage my clients to write the goal, then journal one step at a time. Writing allows us to visually see what is in our minds. Write the vision on index cards. Place them where you visit often: bathroom mirror, refrigerator, closet door, car dashboard.

Creating a vision board is another idea. Yes, bombard your mind with your vision. Allow your vision to speak to you, and in turn, you will speak to your vision. Constant visualization keeps you focused and in step with the process.

"Write the vision, and make it plain upon tablets, that he may run that readeth it. For the vision is yet for an appointed time, but at the end, it shall speak, and not lie."
Habakkuk 2:2-3 (KJV)

Ding, ding, ding, ding. The sound of the bell rings one last time. "Sergeant Major Jones departing," the voice echoes.

"The ceremony is over. I'm retired. What do I do with my life?" said the now military veteran as his voice grew hoarse and his eyes filled with tears.

The certainty of the unknown and the reality of ending this chapter had met him at life's door. There were times when he wanted to leave the military, but circumstances prevented him from doing so. Now, it is time for him to say goodbye, but he longs to stay.

There were key moments he remembered while growing up in Section 8 housing. His mother was on drugs, and food was scarce. He and his younger brother vowed not to join a gang, although that path seemed like the only way to get ahead.

The veteran realized he had to step up, or he would be forever stuck. He did not want to be stuck. Why would anyone want to be in that predicament?

His target was something better. He wanted money. He wanted not to ever be hungry. He wanted to provide for his family. "I didn't know what I was doing joining the military, but I took my chances. I didn't have much to lose," he mumbled.

The distinguished Medal of Valor awardee had heard the words, “Job well done,” many times over the course of his twenty-year service. As tears flooded his aged eyes, the veteran buried his face in his hands and lamented, “What was it all for? I have everything and yet I have nothing. I have given my life. Everyone thinks I am a success. They think I have all the answers, but I feel lost.”

He thought of how proud his wife, kids, mother, and brother were of him. His mother is sober and living well. His brother is a success in his own right. His reputation among his comrades and associates was impressive. Yet, he felt depressed, fearful, and anxious, as if his life had no meaning.

He did not know who he was or who he could become outside the military gates. For years, he had been driven by the military mission and the expectations of others, and he had not discovered his reason for being. The once accomplished feeling of life now felt empty.

Questions like *Who am I? Why am I here? Where did I come from? What was I born to do? What am I capable of? Where do I belong? Why am I different? What is my true potential? Where am I headed?* And why *was I placed on this earth?* They are not just passing thoughts. They are profound, universal questions that stir within the heart of every human being.

These questions are the soul's search for meaning, identity, and destiny. Questions that echo through every stage of life, quietly demanding answers. We must seek the answers to these questions of purpose to enjoy a meaningful, practical, fulfilling, and peaceful life.

Purpose is the Key to Life

Without purpose, life has no meaning. Knowing our purpose in life is essential for setting clear, long-term goals. Setting goals is not just about going about our day-to-day activities. Setting goals must be intentional. You may not get the big picture of life initially, nor will your steps on the journey be without questions. However, ask yourself the tough questions and be willing to be honest with where you are and where you want to be.

How, then, do we set and pursue these goals?

Tell Yourself the Truth

There is no freedom without truth. One of the most significant deceptions in life is deceiving or lying to yourself. Lying to yourself keeps you in bondage, entangled in your past with no hope for a better outcome. Being honest allows you to understand and work within your strengths and limitations. It also allows you to set realistic and attainable goals.

Self-evaluation is a powerful tool for personal growth. Telling yourself the truth involves a process of honest self-assessment and realistic planning. Honest self-reflection involves identifying strengths and weaknesses, setting goals, tracking progress, adjusting, and seeking feedback.

These steps will keep you focused, accountable, and adaptable, ensuring steady progress. If you are not honest with yourself, you may set impossible goals or become discouraged when you cannot meet your high standards.

Take Responsibility for Your Life

Have you ever asked yourself why things are or are not working? Have you made excuses or blamed others for your current stagnation? Blaming people for your mistakes is irresponsible.

Giving excuses is the lifestyle of a mediocre or lazy person. Don't let excuses be your go-to. Don't let excuses extinguish your future. Please note that you are responsible for your life and must make plans to actively and intentionally pursue 'something better.'

Practice Mindfulness

Mindfulness is the practice of paying respectful attention to what's happening both within you and around you. Meditation can help facilitate this process, guiding you through calm, intentional breaths that anchor you in the present moment. As you inhale and exhale with awareness, you quiet the noise and become more attuned to your thoughts, emotions, and surroundings.

This clarity fosters greater self-awareness, helps you refocus on your goals, and empowers you to take purposeful steps forward. In a world filled with constant motion, mindfulness and meditating on what truly matters can be the very antidote to the chaos of everyday life.

Target Deadline

Set a target date by which you want to complete your goal. Sometimes we carry goals and purposes that are more challenging and require more time. In that case, create a step-by-step process and attach a cutoff time for completion.

I personally like this method because it allows for the celebration of small steps, and in return, the significant objective becomes more attainable. When you go in blindly, you may find yourself working on several projects but never completing any of them. Burnout can come quickly.

The fear of failure may begin to set in. It is when you focus on your target and take responsibility for every step that you will feel success, measured in personal satisfaction.

Now, let's see how being optimistic can add value to our destiny and purpose. Read on!

Chapter Three Questions

Defining Target

1. It takes courage to tell yourself the truth. What hard things are you willing to admit to yourself about yourself, or your present situation?

2. What areas/actions in your life have you not taken full responsibility for?

3. Abandon the victim's mentality. Think of a situation you were in that produced a negative outcome on your life. How did you contribute to this? What will you do about it now and for future situations?

Chapter 4

2nd Principle–Be Optimistic

When I examined Merriam-Webster's definition of "optimistic," a lump began to form in my throat. It says, "Feeling or showing hope for the future." It is a factor that, no matter what you see or how bad things have become, it is essential to hold on to hope and believe that it will get better.

The lump in my throat came from the thought that many people have given up on life. Some have committed suicide, thinking that nothing good can happen to them. Still, I firmly believe that 'something better' is coming. I have the faith of a grain of a mustard seed to believe in better days.

Do you know how tiny a mustard seed is? About one millimeter in diameter. That is about the size of a sharpened pencil or crayon point. This significant speck of faith will take one from a world of doubt to a life of fulfillment, regretting nothing.

"Be Optimistic" is more than just a mantra; it is a principle that can transform your life and help you get the most out of it. Optimism is believing that successful things will happen, and challenges will work out. This mindset does not mean ignoring life's problems but approaching them with hope and positivity.

Have you encountered “What if" people? These people want to embark on ‘something better’ in life but live in fear and doubt. When presented with a different perspective or adventure, the first question is, "What if?" Yes, one should expect some questions. However, do not camp out in the "What if?"

"What if I start the business and customers don't come?"

"What if I take my time and write the business proposal, yet it is rejected?"

"What if I lose all my money in the process?"

Every goal has limits, but constantly questioning things can hinder forward movements. Do not concentrate on disadvantages. Dwelling on one's limitations disrupts progress. Instead, highlight the good and solve problems as they arise. Invert the negative of "What if it doesn't work" to ask yourself, "What if it does work?"

The start-up business, the business proposal, and the contract you are looking for might be a challenging win, but have you tried? Experiences run differently, but despite that, the day you put your best foot forward may be the day of your lifting.

One thing that guarantees success is consistency. One thing that guarantees failure is giving up or not trying. It may take time, but you will win when you keep trying.

See Every Challenge as a Stepping Stone

Like a traveler, smooth roads come, but along the path are rocks, dips, and potholes. Still, will you remain in the vehicle until you reach your destination? Or will you turn around to avoid the road less traveled?

Whether you fly on a plane or sail on a ship, every means of transportation has its own particular challenges. So it is with life; whether you are born with a silver spoon or a wooden spoon, you will always experience challenges on your way to your destination. One thing is sure: if you continue your journey, you will ultimately reach your destination.

That rock or bump may slow you down or set you back, but your journey will not be complete without them. Stay hopeful. One truth I have learned is that when you involve God in your journey, everything around you will work together to ensure you reach your destination. The good, bad, and ugly will all work together for your good. The scripture is true,

"And we know that God causes everything to work together for the good of those who love God and are called according to his purpose for them."
Romans 8:28 (NLT)

I love salsa. My husband likes it spicy hot. I prefer the mild flavor. There will be a distinct taste if you taste the tomatoes, peppers, onions, cilantro, and other ingredients separately. When you combine these ingredients in preparing salsa, you will get a fantastic sauce with a pleasing aroma and flavor. This is not the best analogy, but perhaps it can be understood.

That is how it works with life. God can use all the ingredients, the experiences, good and bad, to prepare a full gourmet meal that will leave you full and satisfied. Something better is for you. Believe that!

Many people have gotten breakthroughs after facing challenges or failures. For instance, Thomas Alva Edison made 1,000 unsuccessful attempts to produce the light bulb. If he had stopped, the invention of the light bulb would have been delayed. But his last efforts produced it. When interviewed, he responded that he didn't fail 1,000 times, but that the light bulb was an invention with 1,000 steps.

Challenges and failures can provide individuals with a deeper understanding of how to improve their approach and achieve better results. Some people will see Edison's attempts as a failure, but he saw it as more insight needed to make the light bulb work. The 1,000 failed attempts became a stepping stone to rediscover the best way to produce the light bulb. Stepping stones are challenges to help one get to their desired dreams. If avoided, one may miss out on experiences that could help them at the next level.

Many people dwell in the past and consequently stunt their personal growth. One should learn from their past yet keep one's eyes forward. Here is what I mean. I love accompanying my husband to his college reunion. We take the four-hour flight to our four-day weekend getaway with hope and excitement.

Seeing former college mates and engaging with his fraternity brothers is one of my husband's highlights of the year. Seeing adult men reminisce about their college years is live entertainment for me.

However, one fraternity brother remains stuck in those college years. Meaning the man could not get past that point. His relationships, we learned, were dormant, and his finances ran accordingly. Thirty years have come and gone.

The college student, once an elite athlete in his former years, became stagnant with his next step and, therefore, has not achieved his goals in life. A person who lives in the past is like someone who consistently chooses to dwell in memories. His past thinking now dominated his present being.

The past teaches you how to avoid making the same mistakes. It helps you navigate current situations with the wisdom that comes only from experience. The past is a designated nurturer if granted permission. Once granted, the present and future will manifest what was in the mind of the dreamer.

Note that not only can bad experiences equip you for the future, but good experiences from the past can serve as an anchor for replicating results. Whether you have good or bad experiences in relationships, business, career, health, or finances, these experiences serve as teachers and provide moral lessons to help you go from valley to mountaintop.

The same result will appear if you resist learning from your previous mistakes. For instance, you are in business with someone who has less skill and experience. You chose the business partnership in hopes not only to teach the business owner but to invest in something you believe in. After investing your capital in the partnership, there were severe losses. With no new strategies to recover the loss, the partnership dissolves.

Over time, someone else presents you with a business proposal. Due to your experience, you should evaluate both the person's and the business's past and present performance. Your evaluation should include the person's skills, years of experience, and the strategies they plan to use (that have been successful in the past) to ensure business success.

In this way, one experience provides the knowledge to help you make necessary adjustments before investing in the business idea. The fact that you were unsuccessful before does not mean you will not be successful this time, if you cross your t's and dot your i's before moving forward.

Do not let your past negatively affect your present and future.

Your past mistakes should not be a yardstick for judgment. The conditions of the past, present, and future is different. A client, whom I will call Clara, had some guilty feelings about how she raised her children. Clara was born in the mid-1940s, and her education was limited to the eleventh grade.

Although Clara received her GED, she found it hard being a single mother raising four children. Her children are now adults, but Clara admitted to feeling guilt, shame, and anger over her past choices during the coaching session. These choices led her to continually seek a better-paying job. Eventually, she sought assistance from the government.

Clara blamed herself for the deficiencies in her self-worth and self-esteem. I instructed her to write five positive things about herself. Then, we evaluated where she is now compared to where she was twenty or thirty years ago. We went back and forth, implementing techniques that painted a better picture of Clara's present and future.

Clara realized she did the best she could in that era of her life. All was not lost. You see, all of Clara's children graduated from high school, and three of them went on to college. All four children had excellent employment opportunities.

Past failures may have been due to the unfavorable conditions of that time. Suppose one continues to look at past failures without learning the lessons it has to offer. In that case, we will never evolve to create a better present or future.

The future is worth the risk. It is time to move forward!

Be a Risk-Taker

People tend to avoid taking risks. It may be the fear of the unknown. Experiences have often prevented people from taking risks and making significant progress. As shared earlier, the past will continuously repeat itself if you choose to do nothing. Remember the "What if" syndrome?

Life itself is entirely risky; if you do not take risks, you will not grow. Watch, seek counsel, and take strategic actions to help you push forward. If you refuse to move, what you are afraid of will hibernate into your next season, which will be the same season you are currently in.

Never give up!

Have you noticed something about people who never give up? They usually get what they want. This attribute is a rare gift that anyone who wants to succeed in any endeavor in life should have.

I saw a video of a man who wanted to climb to a specific mountain height but always fell short of his goal. With each step, the more he tried to get to the top, the more he lost. Instead of remaining on the ground, the man kept trying and eventually reached his destination. What does this tell you?

A quitter never gets there, but the one who refuses to quit, no matter how often he falls, will gain resilience. Friends, stay the course, keep trying, keep learning, keep improving yourself.

You can depend on yourself. Don't let yourself down. Keep seeking counsel from people who have gone ahead of you, and in due time, your name will be among those whose persistence produced results.

During your trying season, be very optimistic and keep your goals ahead of you. Keep your dreams in mind and the failures left behind you. Focus on success (your success, not anyone else's) because what you keep your eyes on will eventually become your reality.

Let optimism be infectious in your life. A positive attitude helps create a supportive environment. This positive social network can provide support when the weight of it all seems unbearable. Optimism can open doors to new opportunities. It encourages you to take risks and pursue your goals with confidence.

Optimism empowers you to see the best life has to offer. Do not allow circumstances to determine your feelings; let your vision of a better tomorrow give you hope and influence for today. Embrace optimism and watch how it cultivates something better.

Chapter Four Questions

Be Optimistic

1. What realities are standing in the way of your dreams?

2. Think about and write down the best possible outcomes for various areas of your life, such as ministry, careers, or relationships. How will you know you have succeeded?

3. What fears do you have about taking risks?

4. Being optimistic requires being grateful. List five things you have been grateful for within the last 30 days.

Chapter 5

3rd Principle–The Pursuit of Knowledge

Knowledge is paramount to anyone wanting something better. To excel, pursue knowledge from successful mentors and impactful resources. Excellence demands continuous learning from wise counsel and relevant materials.

Remember, not every piece of knowledge is for you. Learning various things is very insightful; however, gain knowledge pertinent to your purpose and goals.

We all want to be the best at what we do. Right? Whether it is obtaining a first-class degree, making the most business profit, topping the music charts for a musician, or winning awards as an actor. While everyone craves success, only a few can attain it. What do you think makes the difference between the latter and the former? Knowledge!

As basic as it sounds, knowledge is the key. Two people can operate in the same career but have different results - one is a tremendous success, and the other spirals downward. One is left wondering and pondering...but both are doing the same thing.

How is it that one succeeded, and the other did not? The answer is simple. Knowledge! The presence or lack of it makes the difference.

What do the words "cultivate your craft" mean to you? In my mid-twenties, I had a mentor push me to levels I did not think I would survive. I desired to be an entrepreneur, a Life Coach, and a published author.

First, she taught me to focus on one matter at a time. I concentrated on Life Coaching. I dedicated years to training and volunteering in this field. I read many books and maintained constant practice. I cultivated my craft.

To become an author, I took creative writing classes in college, joined writing groups, read many books, and was persistent in maintaining a writing schedule. Again, I honed my creative skills.

While seeking knowledge, understand that not all information is relevant to you. Discard unnecessary, meaningless information that may cloud your judgment, delay your success, or waste your time. To be successful, one must have an in-depth knowledge of who, what, and how. Let us explore these three areas.

WHO?

From whom am I obtaining this knowledge?

Examine the source. Is the person qualified to educate me on the next level? How can a financially distressed person teach another person to obtain financial freedom? Not just anyone should feed you knowledge; it should be someone with the truth evident by what they teach.

People can only give what they have. Also, even if someone has the result, be careful to ensure that the person is living with integrity. Individuals who achieve success by deceit can only teach others dishonest methods.

WHAT?

What information am I getting from this person?

Information is power! The lack thereof can lead one to be years behind on life's journey. Whatever information one obtains, one should ask whether it is of value and whether it will lead to positive results.

Just because someone shares the same values as you or has specific visible results does not necessarily mean that they will always give you sound advice relevant to your destiny. Therefore, analyze any information and allow wisdom to guide you.

HOW?

How will this information benefit me?

Aspiring to greatness means recognizing the value of every piece of information. But when something offers no benefit to your growth or future, dismiss it without hesitation.

Prioritize what truly matters. Recognize your ability to implement this information and structure the information to fit your goals. Success does not stop with acquiring knowledge. One must practice this knowledge to distinguish what fits and what to discard.

For example, if you read this book and apply its lessons, you may begin to build lasting confidence and a stronger sense of self-worth. This can lead to greater balance of life, clarity of purpose, and ultimately, success in your overall well-being. On the other hand, choosing not to act may mean missing out on a valuable opportunity for growth and transformation—a chance to create the life you were meant to live.

Extinguish the arrival mentality: never stop learning. I have always had the mindset of two necessary antidotes. One, I am a work in progress. And two, I am a lifelong learner.

The fact that one sought knowledge yesterday is not enough. One step at a time, better than yesterday, and aiming to be a better version of oneself should be one's daily mantra.

Those with an arrival temperament are happy with their success and are not looking to improve. They are satisfied with where they are and have no desire for more. The moment one thinks they have arrived, one stops growing. God wants you to be your best, do your best, and share your best throughout your journey.

The best is not a destination. It is a journey. One must be prepared to access knowledge, ready to learn, and willing to take the journey forward.

Chapter Five Questions

The Pursuit of Knowledge

1. Without curiosity, there would be no motivation to learn, explore, or discover. What areas/dreams in your life bring curiosity?

2. What have you sacrificed in the pursuit of knowledge?

3. Who do you know has a learning environment that would benefit your present and future? What steps are you willing to take in pursuit of it?

Chapter 6

4th Principle–Relationship Investments

Every destiny requires support to be fulfilled. No one achieves their purpose alone. If you are on Earth, your journey is meant to involve people, relationships, mentors, encouragers, and even challengers, all woven into the path that leads you to your destination. Some may say, "All I need is God," or "I don't need anyone; I can do it myself." But that mindset, though it may sound strong, is rooted in pride and isolation. It often leads to exhaustion and early burnout. God designed us for connection.

Destiny is rarely a solo pursuit.

God says it this way:

"Then God blessed them, and God said to them, 'Be fruitful and multiply; fill the earth and subdue it; have dominion over the fish of the sea, over the birds of the air, and over every living thing that moves on the earth."
Genesis 1:28 (NKJV)

Likewise,

"Two are better than one because they have a good return for their labor: If either of them falls down, his friend can help him up. But pity the man who falls and has no one to help him up!"
Ecclesiastes 4:9-10 (NIV)

Genesis tells us that God created the Earth and gave it to man to have DOMINION. Here, DOMINION means that God trusted human beings enough to care for the Earth and rule over the affairs of the land. Isn't it something that an all-powerful God trusts a powerless human being? How does that make you feel knowing that God trusts you and me?

For anything to work effectively, one must be fully and actively involved. In your journey to fulfill your destiny, people can either be a hindrance or a gateway. One must decide who they let into their inner circle. If a person is a hindrance, it is time to release the ball and chain and part ways. If one brings value to you, be bold enough to permit them to enter your circle.

Remember, people are in our lives for a season, and some are in our lives for a lifetime. We, you and I, have a choice to keep them there for the appointed times. To highlight a previous point. A young lawyer was knowledgeable and skillful in his business. He graduated from one of the prestigious law schools in the country.

One of the most respected Senior Advocates mentors him. The young lawyer tried his best to connect with the mentor, but his efforts were useless. He sent emails and booked appointments with him. Still, the Senior Advocate was like a prince guarded by a heavy fortress.

One day, the mentor invited the young lawyer to his home, where he and other colleagues were holding a meeting. When the young lawyer arrived, the Senior Advocate asked him to walk alongside him. The young lawyer anticipated a long discussion about the years of experience and journey to success that led the mentor to his current position.

The mentor filled the young lawyer with valuable information about his journey. After the walk, the mentor said, "If your life doesn't change after this, then you are not ready for the big stage."

From that day on, the young lawyer adjoined with his mentor in the courtroom and the office. When people saw the Mentor, they also saw the mentee. It was as if they were joined at the hip.

The young lawyer's career flourished, and his name became known throughout the city. Years later, the now-seasoned lawyer prepared himself to assume the Senior Advocate's position upon the retirement of his mentor.

This story tells us that someone has already attained the height you are aspiring to, and it is vital that you establish relationships with people at that level. Learn to build strong communication skills that will help you maintain your relationships.

Be respectful and patient with all leadership instructions. In the young lawyer's case, if he had arrogantly told the senior advocate, 'I didn't travel this far to take a stroll with you,' he would have missed an opportunity.

The way and manner which you relate to people matters. Be careful not to use the physical looks of a person to judge their ability to shift your life for the better. People are the links to what you need; some embody the wisdom you need, and others may encompass sound relationships that are paramount to your career's growth.

When God gives you the privilege to be associated with people of that caliber, resist the urge to undervalue the relationship; always ensure you respect and honor them. Honor opens the doors of access for whoever you align with.

Above all, remember gratitude. Thanking people encourages them to help more. Learn to not only speak but also act on the words 'THANK YOU.' Many people have closed their doors to greater heights because of their inability to express their appreciation to someone who helped them.

On your journey through life, never leave a 'Thank you' without voice or action. These two words, when practiced habitually, hold powerful meanings that brace you to see everything in a different light.

Chapter Six Questions

Relationship Investment

1. It is important to examine the relationship you have with yourself. Would you speak to someone else or care for someone else the way you speak or care for yourself? Why or why not?

2. In what ways could you cultivate positive/meaningful relationships in the following areas?

a) Quality time

b) Be present

c) Active Listening

d) Recognize unhealthy relationships

Chapter 7

5th Principle–Effective Discipline

Discipline is self-control gained by requiring that rules or orders be obeyed. It is the ability to keep working at something difficult. If being the best at your work is your aim, then you must embrace discipline. Apostle Paul wrote:

"No discipline seems pleasant at the time, but painful. Later on, however, it produces a harvest of righteousness and peace for those who have been trained by it."
Hebrews 12:11 (NLT)

Let this become a standard for your life. Will it be easy? Of course not. Would it be worth it? Definitely! Discipline requires time management, organization, without procrastination. Let's review each one.

Value Time Management

Time Management is an essential quality of self-discipline. Seconds turn into hours, hours roll into days, days into weeks, weeks become months, months turn into years, and years make up a lifetime. Each passing time is significant to the fulfillment of your destiny.

Suppose you spend most of your time doing things that are not beneficial to your future. Chances are, you may never live up to the full manifestation of who God desired you to be when he created you.

Time is an expensive commodity. Once lost, time cannot be regained. As much as everyone would love to take a break and have a leisurely experience, rest, and have fun, you should make the most of the time available.

Having a weekly, quarterly, and yearly assessment helps you understand what you are spending your time on, how valuable and essential it is, and how it has contributed to making you a better person.

Regardless of your economic status, you cannot repurchase time. I cannot stress this statement enough. It is important to remember that the goal of each day is to be better than the day before.

You can easily get lost in the hustle and bustle of life and career as we strive to survive and support our loved ones and friends. However, maintaining a balanced life is rooted in effective time management.

Your purpose should be your driving force. What you did or achieved during the day, the time spent doing it, and how it will impact your world should contribute to your assessment.

Be Organized

Order and organization wash each other's hands. One must prioritize, organize, and set goals. Consider maintaining a to-do list or a daily calendar.

Having a daily schedule and checking off the 'tasks done' box motivates you to press forward. Set targets of things you wish to accomplish daily, weekly, or monthly, as you deem fit.

Orderliness can significantly enhance your appearance and appeal. Whether at home, in the office, or at school, keeping your belongings and yourself organized reflects your character.

Living in disorder takes more energy, physically and mentally, than one is willing to admit. Additionally, this technique maximizes your time, making it more productive and allowing more time for leisure.

Overcome Procrastination

Procrastination is a waste of time and often a symptom of laziness. For discipline to work, you must avoid procrastination. Why do tomorrow what you can do today?

When you plan to do something at a particular time, ensure you do it at the scheduled time. Make an appointment with yourself. Pen it in on your calendar and do not cancel unless it is a true emergency, I repeat, a true emergency that warrants a delay.

When we procrastinate, we delay our progress and our blessings. Diligence, consistency, and hard work yield results and success. Diligence and procrastination cannot work side by side. No one wants to do business with a procrastinator—one whose 9:00 a.m. ends up being 1:00 p.m. One who promises to deliver a service on Monday but by Thursday still needs time to prepare.

You can be gifted, talented, highly skilled, and yet not sought after because one cannot be trusted to fulfill commitments. People will not take you seriously if they cannot hold you to your word.

There are 86,400 seconds in a day, and God plans for us to use that time wisely. Inactivity causes you to lose the reward of the fruits of your labor. You must intentionally apply discipline in all aspects of your life. Success is inevitable when preparation meets hard work.

Chapter Seven Questions

Effective Discipline

1. Where is most of your time devoted?

2. How does setting boundaries fit your basic priorities?

3. What planning tools, i.e. calendars, notebooks, phone apps, Dictaphone, charts, have you used to improve your time management? In what ways has this been helpful?

4. Procrastination can be habit-forming. What dreams/goals/tasks have you delayed and long to achieve?

Chapter 8

6th Principle–A Still Place Within

No matter how successful you become or what you achieve, you lose if you do not have joy and peace of mind. Getting the best out of life necessitates that achievements ensure happiness and peace, and that you remain intact. Life is more than having things. The greatest assets in life are not material, but intangible assets, such as joy, peace, a happy family, good relationships, soundness of mind, and more.

Whatever you acquire in life at the expense of others, you have truly gained little. Unfortunately, some wealthy people take their lives due to a lack of one or more of these aspects. Many arrive at success unaware of the battles it holds.

Success, at any level, will attract many people, including those who are haters. At this time, you must stay grounded, surround yourself with people who can help shield the fiery darts, and, most of all, maintain your inner peace.

You may ask, "Why on Earth will someone with so much wealth, influence, and fame get depressed or take their life?

What does one lack? The answer lies within. Yes, having prosperity is good. Sustaining prosperity is a sacrifice.

"Beloved, I pray that you may prosper in all things and be in health, just as your soul prospers."
3 John 2 (NKJV)

God wants you to prosper more than you want it yourself. Not just financially, he desires for you to thrive in every area of your life. When you are happy with yourself and have inner peace, any mountain can be readily overcome.

What is money if you do not have love?

What is love if one does not have peace?

Practice Forgiveness

First and foremost, I will say that as sure as you and I are breathing, offenses will come. It's a fact of life.

"Things that cause people to stumble are bound to come, but woe to anyone through whom they come."
Luke 17:1 (NIV)

The stumbling blocks Jesus is talking about here are offenses. The first key to ensuring you do not lose joy and peace of mind is to learn to forgive people when they offend you.

Living with anger, bitterness, envy, or the like is not wise. Think of the ball and chain discussed earlier. These things are designed to slow your progress, leading to stagnation.

In my book, *Why Not Forgive: An Action Plan for Peace and Freedom,* I provide practical steps to help you implement forgiveness on your journey. Understand that you are not forgiving the person who wronged you for their own sake. Instead, it releases you from the bondage of unforgiveness.

Can you calculate how often you get offended in a day? Or how about a month? If forgiveness is delayed, an unhealthy and aggressive response may arise within you due to the internal hurt.

Unforgiveness can carry over into every area of your life. You may think it is not a problem until you lash out at your spouse or children without cause. If there is no peace within you, there is no peace in your family because you are an integral part of your family's unit.

If you have any grievances against someone, please let them go today and be free. Forgive those who offend you even when they do not deserve it or never ask for your forgiveness. Forgive them, for your sake.

Be Patient, Seasons Change

Geography teaches us that the Earth rotates on its axis and revolves around the Sun simultaneously. Due to the change in the sun's position, we have day and night. Therefore, it will not always be dark days.

The situation you are in now may or may not be a dark place. It may be difficult to bear, but do not let it steal your time, peace, or joy. Just as it has come into your life, it will surely pass. But you must remain patient. I understand patience does not come naturally for any of us. Patience is a valuable virtue that requires trust in God's timing.

"Be patient in tribulation, be constant in prayer,"
Romans 12:12 (NIV)

Patience is not waiting while complaining. It is waiting with calmness, optimism, faith, and knowledge that your predicament will change. Your season will change like the seasons of fall, winter, spring, and summer. Your predicament does not define your purpose, nor does it determine your destiny.

"It won't be like this always," my mother told us. Those words became a guiding light to me as an eight-year-old girl. Growing up, there was my mother, siblings, and I. My mother dropped out of high school but was successful at getting her GED. However, she was divorced by the time she was twenty-seven.

Being poor was an everyday reality for us. We moved from house to house in the same neighborhood because my mother could not afford the increase in rent.

I remember one winter day when we ran out of firewood. My mother sent my brother, sister, and me into the woods to gather limbs to burn in our wood heater. This is the same wood heater we would use to heat water to take a bath. The same wood heater we would use to cook when our gas was empty.

My mother looked all her children in the eye, then looked at the floor, and moving her head from side to side, said, "It won't be like this always. Be patient; our change is coming." I get a lump in my throat and tears in my eyes because she was right. It took some years, but our change came.

What keeps you through hard times? Your path can take many turns, but if you study the lives of successful people, you will discover that patience played a significant role in their success.

"Let patience have its perfect work, that you may be perfect and complete, lacking nothing."
James 1:3-4 (NKJV)

Sometimes, it takes patience to see a turnaround in one's circumstances. And when patience has "its perfect work," prosperity is close at hand.

Chapter Eight Questions

A Still Place Within

1. What peace does this passage bring to you?

"Forgive us our sins, for we also forgive everyone who sins against us..."
Luke 11:4 (NIV)

2. What offenses are you holding on to that you need to release?

3. Change is continuous and a natural part of life. What changes have occurred in your/family life that called for readjustments?

4. Are you aware of the season of life you're in right now? What attributes of faith are being asked of you in this moment—is it trust, confidence, surrender, obedience, perseverance, or something deeper?

Chapter 9

7th Principle–Life Balances

In our pursuit of happiness and success, it's easy to get caught up in the grind of everyday life. Ambition takes over, and we begin to measure our worth by how busy we are or how much we've achieved. However, when we focus too much on one area, such as work or wealth, we often neglect our health, relationships, and inner peace.

Without realizing it, we sacrifice the very things that make life worth living. A balanced life doesn't mean we stop reaching goals; it means we pursue them with a clear mind, a whole heart, and steady priorities.

Balance is about more than just juggling responsibilities. It's a way of living that values harmony between work, family, health, personal growth, and rest. Each of these play an important part in our happiness and long-term well-being. When one area is constantly neglected, everything else eventually suffers.

Making time for rest and reflection strengthens our resilience. Investing in loved ones deepens our sense of purpose. Nurturing our body and mind strengthens our ability to meet the pressures of a driven life. Balance isn't a luxury. It's a requirement for a meaningful life.

True balance reaches into every area: spiritual, physical, financial, and emotional. It keeps us grounded when life pulls us in different directions. It helps us say no to what drains us and yes to what fuels us.

When our lives are aligned, we're not just surviving, we're thriving. Stress is decreased, clarity increases, and joy becomes more consistent. We don't just chase success; we're able to enjoy it. A balanced life is one where we're fully present, deeply connected, and prepared for both the wins and the challenges that lie ahead.

Balance in Work and Rest

While putting in a lot of effort is necessary to reach our goals, working nonstop without enough rest is dangerous. It's synonymous with signing a contract with an untimely death. Rest isn't a reward, it's a requirement.

The demands of life are intense and overwhelming. Let us face it, we live in a world that makes it hard for one to really unwind. This should not be. Our goal should be to prevent burnout. We can never be healthy enough without adequate rest.

Rest is medicine. It promotes healing and rejuvenates our minds. Our creativity is regenerated, our strength replenished, and our productivity increases as our bodies have been energized by rest.

It is tough for some people to turn off work mode. I am guilty as charged. When I served in the military, I was always on guard. If you ask any former military or those in high-powered professions, they'll tell you it's hard to turn on the body's relaxation mechanism, even when the danger or pressure is long gone.

Sometimes one may feel uncomfortable or guilty about relaxing. Nevertheless, practicing regular breaks, ensuring sufficient sleep, and scheduling leisure time are important. Sleep is a must; it is not a luxury. It serves as the cornerstone for long-term innovation and productivity.

For the past 15 years, I've made it a discipline to set aside one day each week for self-care. I detox my body through fasting, refresh my mind with meditation and reflection, and often unwind with a good book. I also intentionally power down my phone, so I'm not tempted by the pings, beeps, or glowing notifications demanding my attention.

Additionally, I make a point to take time to rest and de-stress at least twice a year. Depending on what's going on, I usually spend seven to 10 days away from home. I also take a couple of weekend getaways! Then, I take a three-month sabbatical, also known as furlough, every four to five years.

During the sabbatical, I intentionally reflect on where I am and where I am going. I access my personal life, spiritual life, career, and goals without the pressure of making quick decisions. I re-prioritize as necessary.

Balance in Personal and Professional Life

Many people focus more on their work and spend less time with their families as a sacrifice to achieve success. The other is where parents are at home but do not pay much attention to their children. I have seen both sides.

Growing up in a single-parent family, my mother had to work. She implemented chores for all her children, which took a lot of pressure off her. She made the most of the quality time we had together.

That is what matters!

Are you making the most of your time and not allowing life's busyness to zap your energy to the point one has nothing left?

Do the people near and dear to you feel seen, heard, valued, and loved?

Are loved ones aware and included in your aspirations?

The relevance of including your family in your goals helps to balance the pages of success. I remember our family meetings. Mother would talk to us about family finances (or the lack thereof) and other vital life issues.

By doing this, we children understood why we could not have things other kids in our neighborhood or school had. We would not ask our mother for new clothes or shoes. I am sure it bothered her, but we knew not asking also brought relief.

Parents should involve their families in the pursuit of their goals. While children may not contribute much to the workload, they can offer encouragement, joy, and a sense of unity. Too often, parents feel they don't have time to play with their children, engage in their interests, or stay connected with what's happening in their lives.

This disconnect usually stems from an inability to balance personal and professional responsibilities. Over time, that imbalance can create unnecessary tension in both marriage and family life. Small moments of connection can make a big difference.

It is crucial to spend quality time with family and friends. These connections offer happiness, emotional support, and a feeling of community. They are the cornerstone of a happy existence. One can acquire everything in this life and lose one's family, soul, and overall well-being. One will still long to be satisfied and feel empty and lonely inside.

Having success in our careers is okay, but not if it comes at the expense of our relationships. Engaging in social events, planning regular family time, and staying in the moment with our loved ones guarantee we always keep sight of the essential things in life.

Balance in Physical and Mental Health

I understand one wants to "Make it big" in life. Still, one's physical and psychological well-being should not take a back seat. Learning to check in with oneself and becoming self-aware of the physical discomforts in one's body often tells us we are taking on more than we can handle.

Cheryl had accomplished so much in her forty years of life. She was a wife, mother, entrepreneur, and professor. One day, her body began to tense up, and she had a headache that caused her nausea. Her appointment with her doctor revealed stress, high blood pressure, fatigue, and muscle weakness. "Sounds like your reserves are tapped out," said her doctor, "your body is trying to tell you something."

Many of us are guilty of this, particularly now, as we strive to keep up with a fast-paced society. We learn to override physical discomfort in the name of productivity. Overworking your body to the point of total exhaustion can lead to physical breakdown. Our bodies are not machines; they are designed to rest.

Our body is talking to us. Are we listening?

Neglecting your health can have long-term effects that lead to sickness, depression, and could cause your goals to be delayed or unfulfilled. Brain fog, high blood pressure, fatigue, and headaches are warning sirens we often dismiss. Then, there are changes in your behavior.

According to research conducted by the Cleveland Clinic, the following are red flags leading to the body's physical and mental debilitation:

- Your sleep is off kilter
- You skip meals or do not eat or drink enough
- You are not getting enough exercise
- You consume substances like drugs or alcohol when overwhelmed
- You neglect meaningful relationships
- Overall, you stop taking care of yourself

An untimely death from being overworked does not happen overnight; it slowly accumulates over the years. Eventually, the problem of being a workaholic and the ill health it begets will continue if we do not consciously create balance.

Physical and mental well-being, achieved through hobbies, mindfulness, meditation, regular exercise, and a balanced diet, is crucial to one's present and future. This list enables you to possess the vitality, concentration, and fortitude necessary to overcome life's obstacles. Never damage your health to achieve success; the cost may be too high to sustain your life.

Balance in Giving and Receiving

Understanding the principles of giving and receiving to inherit a balanced life seems counterintuitive. Yet, it works. Humans are self-centered by nature. In other words, it takes conscious practice to be generous.

Have you ever felt that warm, fuzzy feeling after volunteering or donating to a worthy cause? You felt like what you did really made an impact. That is your brain's glimmer and your heart's stirring.

Giving freely of your time, money, and abilities, when done regularly, boosts your stamina and enhances your well-being. Generosity often leads to reciprocity. It is an ancient principle that when you give, you will receive multiples of the measure with which you gave.

You will receive whatever you provide: money, love, mercy, help, etc. This equilibrium ensures that we do not exhaust ourselves, thereby allowing us to continue making meaningful contributions to others. Luke notes:

"Give, and you will receive. Your gift will return to you in full, pressed down, shaken together to make room for more, running over, and poured into your lap. The amount you give will determine the amount you get back."
Luke 6:38 (NLT)

Balance Fun and Play

What stops most people from enjoying themselves?

Why does taking time for fun and play make one feel guilty?

Is it because our self-worth is tied to our careers, productivity, and profitability?

Or is it that we cannot find time for self-care in lieu of adulting?

Fun and play are essential to your mental and physical health. Whenever you do things that make you laugh or help you forget about life's stressors, it rewards both your mind and body. It reminds us that, right now, living is more than just reaching production quotas.

It is about enjoying the journey. Busyness happens. However, we shouldn't let the weight of responsibilities and obligations overshadow the joy and fun life has to offer.

Instead of thinking that having fun is selfish, rethink fun as a preventative measure. In the article, *The Benefits of Play for Adults*, scientists performed subjective studies that summarize the mental and physical benefits of having fun. Some of the benefits include:

- Release endorphins and decrease stress hormones
- It gives your mind a break
- Promotes creativity
- Improves relationships and creates a sense of belonging
- Increase happiness, which protects from depression
- Increase cognitive abilities, in some cases
- Increase energy drained by stress

Remember, fun and play for one may not be fun and play for another. There is no need for comparison. Discover what is truly fun for you and indulge healthily. Commit to making time to play, have fun, and reap the benefits of self-care and love.

Money Has Its Place

Many people inherit their beliefs about money from their parents and grandparents. Often, generational attitudes toward spending, saving, and debt are passed down without question. Gaining insight into these inherited money beliefs can be the first step toward making wiser financial decisions and easing financial stress.

Money does buy many things, but I do not believe money answers all things. True love and peace are priceless and cannot be purchased with cash. However, money does have its place.

Most people need to understand the importance of money in achieving their goals and fulfilling their destiny. Remember: you cannot fulfill destiny and your purpose in poverty, nor with a poverty mentality. For all intents and purposes, a poor person's mindset will remain poor until they choose to change.

King Solomon explains it this way:

A poor, wise man knew how to save the town, and so it was rescued. But afterward, no one thought to thank him. So even though wisdom is better than strength, those who are wise will be despised if they are poor. What they say will not be appreciated for long.
Ecclesiastes 9:15-16 (NLT)

According to the text, two things hinder the poor wise man's contribution to his community. First, his wisdom is despised and dismissed by those who judge its value based on his economic status. How many are guilty of this? Not seeing past the poverty.

Secondly, “His words are not heard.” Put another way, though his words were advantageous, his means limited his reach.

It is possible to change the way you think about money. First, identify and understand the money beliefs that stunt your ability to gain wealth. Next, take those beliefs and adapt to change.

In this aspect, let us look at the wise poor man: it was not only his outer appearance. If the wise poor man has such wisdom to save a city, why would he not use that wisdom professionally to create a better life for himself?

The point here is that you should be intentional about breaking out of poverty and lack. Your best life demands it.

How do you do that?

Review Chapter 5 again: Pursue after Knowledge, pause for a moment, then take steps to persevere through.

The easiest way to learn what you do not know is to ask and learn from those who know it, rather than using the method of trial and error. Tai Lopez, a successful entrepreneur and author, set the thirty-three percent rule.

The rule states to spend 33% of your time with people who have not attained your level--those you can mentor and guide, 33% with your peers--those on the same level as you, and 33% with people who are 10, 20 or even 30 years ahead of where you want to be–those people one can emulate.

There must be a balance. Too much time spent with people below your level can hurt one's mindset. Too much time spent with people above your level can hinder relationships below or at one's level, causing you to alienate the people who have helped you along the way. Finally, always remember those in need. Giving back creates a better you and a better world.

Let money have its proper place. When one has more of it, one can do more with it. When it comes to your work-life balance, physical-mental health, and personal growth-leisure, the rule of 33% can help you create balance and achieve success.

Chapter 9 Questions

Life Balances

1. How effective are you across different life domains? What are you achieving?

a) Faith/Spirituality

b) Job/Career/Education

c) Relationships

d) Health/Physical/Emotional well-being

e) Finances

2. How well do your investments in each area align with your values and priorities?

a) Faith/Spirituality

b) Job/Career/Education

c) Relationships

d) Health/Physical/Emotional well-being

e) Finances

Chapter 10

Legacy of Tomorrow

In the fabric of life, the threads we weave now become the legacy we leave behind tomorrow. The essence of who we are extends beyond the material and into the realms of inspiration, influence, and lasting impact. As we embark on life's journey, we must consider the lessons we teach the next generation and the imprints we leave behind.

Living a Life Worth Emulating

Achieving personal success is not the only measure of a life worth emulating. A truly impactful life is shaped by the principles we uphold, the values we live by, and the compassion we extend to others. It's not just about reaching goals, it's about how we treat people along the way and what kind of legacy we leave behind.

Consider the enduring influence of individuals like Myles Munroe, Billy Graham, and Maya Angelou. Although they are no longer with us, their words, teachings, and example continue to shape the hearts and minds of future generations. Their books, messages, and insights ensure that a life anchored in purpose can leave a legacy that continues to speak long after the person is gone.

The Importance of Training the Next Generation

Training and mentoring others, especially our children, are among the most effective strategies for guaranteeing a better legacy. Achieving success but failing to impart morals and discipline to our children is a grave mistake. Our children and the people we influence in life are the ones who will carry on our ideals and values.

I hasten to continue without mentioning a poem that profoundly affected me as a parent when I began raising my children. Dorothy Law Nolte was a prolific writer, speaker, lifelong teacher, and lecturer on family life education. In 1954, she penned these words:

Children Learn What They Live

Dorothy Law Nolte

If children live with criticism, they learn to condemn.
If children live with hostility, they learn to fight.
If children live with ridicule, they learn to be shy.
If children live with shame, they learn to feel guilty.
If children live with encouragement, they learn confidence.
If children live with tolerance, they learn to be patient.
If children live with praise, they learn to appreciate.
If children live with acceptance, they learn to love.

If children live with approval, they learn to like themselves.
If children live with honesty, they learn truthfulness.
If children live with security, they learn to have faith in themselves and others.
If children live with friendliness, they learn the world is a nice place in which to live.

The message is clear: children are constantly learning from their parents, every single day. Your children are paying close attention, not so much to the instructions you give, but to the actions you model. Parents, you are your child's first and most influential role model. The way you live speaks louder than anything you say.

In today's world, social media and celebrity culture add pressure and distraction, but your example still carries the most significant weight. What they see in you helps shape who they believe they can become.

Parenting also requires mentoring. Allow children to practice what you teach them, and when they make mistakes, correct them in love and encourage them to try again. Let your legacy live on through them.

What we do now will have a ripple effect, positive or negative. For this cause, intentional deeds and instruction must perpetuate our ideals, accomplishments, and beliefs.

We must devote our time, money, and affection to raising the next generation.

Do not die with the knowledge you have within you. Be the seed planter and watch the fruit of your knowledge grow in every season. Could you pass your knowledge on in some way? You could write a poem like Dorothy Law Nolte did, or write a book like I did. You can be creative in the ways you share your knowledge with others.

Dorothy's words live through her children and grandchildren. Present and future generations should be uplifted with purpose and diligence. What we achieve and the values we leave behind for those who follow us define our legacy.

In this digital age, making positive videos is another way to share your knowledge with those close to your heart. A friend who had breast cancer shared that she was creating videos for her then eight-year-old daughter as a remembrance of her.

She created videos about cooking, dating, puberty (including menstrual health), financing on a budget, and other aspects of growing into adulthood. Following my friend's passing, her husband waited for the right time to share the videos with their daughter—each one a piece of her legacy.

What an impact my friend made on her daughter's life.

Be an Example

Our actions teach children and young adults more than words. Leading a life characterized by honesty, faith, endurance, and purpose provides a robust model for children to emulate.

Instill Values

Teaching fundamental concepts like honesty, diligence, empathy, perseverance, and resilience helps ensure these values are birthed and have the space and time to be nurtured. They encourage one another with anecdotes and historical lessons that firmly support these principles.

Offer Education and Opportunities

It is essential to ensure that the next generation has access to education and opportunities to enhance their skills. Because of our empowerment, they can carry on our traditions and leave their mark on society.

Promote Independent Thinking

We are called to equip the next generation to think for themselves and boldly walk the path God lays before them. Times have changed and continue to change. What worked twenty years ago may still hold value, but only as a teaching tool, not a standard to live by.

God is doing a "*new thing*" (Isaiah 43:19), and it requires fresh vision, renewed faith, and unleashed creativity. As mentors, parents, and leaders, we must encourage young minds not to fear change but to embrace it with wisdom and discernment.

Let's raise a generation unafraid to think differently, trust deeply, and create boldly for His glory.

Support and Mentorship

Relentless support and mentorship provide the direction and inspiration needed to overcome life's obstacles. Being a trustworthy advisor and source of knowledge upholds the morals we want to instill in others.

The lives we touch and the generations we affect are the true testaments to our legacy. We ensure that our influence lasts long after we are gone by leading an example-worthy life and carefully educating the next generation.

Our lives can leave a lasting legacy that influences the future, just as the words and deeds of great leaders in history have done. Let us work to leave a legacy for tomorrow, one in which our influence endures over the ages and improves the planet for everyone.

Let your life not just be about something but be used by God to bring about something greater.

Live with purpose.

Walk in obedience.

Be a vessel for **Something Better.**

"For we are God's masterpiece. He has created us anew in Christ Jesus, so we can do the good things He planned for us long ago."
Ephesians 2:10 (NLT)

Chapter Ten Questions

Legacy of Tomorrow

1. You might be surprised who is watching how you live your life. Who are you setting an example for?

2. This generation is hungry for direction, advice, and shared experiences. How can you inject a snippet of your voice into this generation?

3. If someone observed your life closely, would they find that your words back up your lifestyle?

4. What are some ways you can find your legacy in how you live?

5. What are some things that might hinder you from being able to leave the legacy you want? Prioritize these obstacles based on the likelihood of their occurrence and their importance if they do happen.

6. What will your final blessing be?

Chapter 11

Conclusion

Loving ourselves and embracing life as a gift connects us to the abundance and prosperity of our Creator. This is more than a season of change. It is a divine invitation to shape your own destiny. You are not just a character in someone else's script. You are the author of your story. Let life fill its pages with meaning, growth, and transformation.

The choices and changes you make today will set the tone for the life you live tomorrow. Opportunities are present. Possibilities are unfolding. The future is not fixed. Your faith forms it, your actions, and your willingness to believe that something better truly exists for you.

You are not here to compete. You are here to create. There is no one exactly like you. It's time to stop comparing, stop shrinking, and stop settling. Rise into your identity, your purpose, and your God-given design.

Throughout this book, we explored powerful truths about identity, purpose, healing, and intentional living. We talked about what it means to truly become—to heal from the inside out, to step into wholeness, and to choose faith over fear. You were reminded that your past, your mistakes, or the opinions of others do not define your worth. You were encouraged to realign your thoughts, renew your perspective, and recognize the divine potential already within you.

You learned that healing is not a passive process. It is a conscious decision to rise, to let go, and to embrace the lessons that pain and pressure often bring. You have discovered the power of walking in self-awareness, choosing stillness, and listening to the inner voice that God has placed within you.

Now, as we close, I want to leave you with a recap of the seven principles that have guided this journey to Something Better:

The 7 Principles to Living Something Better

Know Your Worth

You are fearfully and wonderfully made. Nothing about your existence is a mistake. Knowing your worth changes how you love, how you heal, and how you walk into your future.

Heal What Hurt You

Pain that is not addressed will repeat itself. Healing is not weakness—it is wisdom. It is the foundation of your strength.

Protect Your Peace

Your peace is sacred. Guard it from chaos, comparison, and emotional vampires. Protecting your peace allows clarity to lead and wisdom to grow.

Practice Mindfulness and Presence

What you pay attention to shapes your reality. Slow down. Be present. Learn to breathe again, to notice beauty again, and to live again.

Embrace Purpose Over Perfection

Perfection is an illusion. Purpose is the path. Stop waiting to have it all together and start living with intention today.

Let God Lead

Trust His timing. Trust His plan. Let Him into the places you've tried to manage alone. Divine alignment is greater than forced outcomes.

Pursue Progress, Not Comparison

Your race is not theirs. You're not behind. You're not late. Growth is sacred, and your only competition is the version of you that stopped believing.

These principles are not quick fixes. They are daily decisions. They are seeds planted by faith and watered by discipline, trust, and grace. If you apply even one of these consistently, you will begin to see change. Apply them all, and your life will reflect a harvest of something better than you've ever imagined.

As I bring this book to a close, I do so with the hope that each chapter has offered you something real. Whether strength in a storm, peace in confusion, or clarity in chaos, I pray these words have been like bread on your journey. May they sustain you, comfort you, and encourage you when life becomes overwhelming or the path seems unclear.

Before you go, I leave you with three powerful quotes, a scripture to meditate on, and a poem written from my heart to yours. These have spoken to me deeply in my own journey toward Something Better. I believe they will speak to you too.

"I will spend a few years living like nobody else will, so I can spend the rest of my life living like nobody else can."
Dr. Boyce Watkins

"Sacrifice really means giving up something good for something better." Stephen R. Covey

"As I look back on my life I realized every time I thought I was being rejected from something good, I was actually being redirected to something better."
Steve Maraboli

"…since God had planned something better for us so that only together with us would they be made perfect."
Hebrews 11:40 (NIV)

Something Better

Eyes wide open, something better is on the rise,
One moment, one mistake, you have a lifetime to shine.
Great influencers plant your seed. The harvest is vast,
One seed planted and watered; the sun will do the rest.

To break through the soil, the seed must press on and fight.
The struggle is real, but I can feel the warmth of light.
Still feed me, cultivating my surrounding atmosphere,
Where I, too, can be a beacon to those who are near.

That something better is for me, as I grow and release my seed,
To the rest of the world, not just in words, but in acts of deed.
Empowering others to something better, not just for today,
But for tomorrow's generation, lest chaff of wheat in the wind,
I easily stray away.

~ Dr. Cassie J Williams

Love yourself, love your life.

You deserve…

SOMETHING BETTER!

A Final Prayer of Blessing

Heavenly Father,

Thank You for the one holding this book. Thank You for their life, their story, and the divine purpose You've planted within them. I lift them up to You now, asking for Your guidance, Your peace, and Your unwavering love to flood their heart.

May they walk boldly into their "something better" with faith, courage, and clarity. May they release what no longer serves them and embrace the life You've prepared for them. Let every seed of hope sown through these pages take root, grow strong, and bear fruit.

Bless their relationships, health, finances, and the work of their hands. Guide their feet as they go. And bless their mind with the peace that surpasses understanding.

May they know that they are enough.

May they always know that they are loved, chosen, and never forgotten.

In Jesus' name,
Amen.

About the Author

Dr. Cassie J. Williams is a retired Navy veteran, ordained minister, and chaplain who passionately empowers women and children through life coaching, mentorship, and spiritual development.

Born into a low-income family, Cassie faced early life challenges following her parents' divorce. She enlisted in the military and pursued higher education, earning a B.S. in Business Administration from Columbia College, a Master's in Theological Studies from Liberty University, and a PhD in Psychology with a Biblical Basis from Dayspring Christian University.

As a certified life coach and anger resolution therapist, she connects deeply with diverse audiences nationwide. She ministers in prisons, Dream Centers, and Saafe Houses. Combining practical life skills with spiritual wisdom, empowering attendees to integrate biblical principles into everyday challenges.

Alongside her husband, Darell, Cassie co-founded Omega Star Ministries to inspire youth through athletic coaching and adults to help them transform their lives.

Dedicated to fostering resilience and self-worth, Dr. Williams champions empowerment as the core of her message. She is a dynamic motivational speaker and Bible teacher actively seeking opportunities to speak and share her inspiring journey. She and her family reside in Central Texas.

Connect with the Author

Thank you for reading *Something Better*. It is truly an honor to share this message of healing, hope, and transformation with you. If these words resonated with your heart or if you're ready to pursue your own "something better," I'd love to stay connected.

Whether you are looking for encouragement, coaching, prayer support, or would like to invite me to speak at your event, I'm here to walk alongside you.

Stay Connected:

Website: https://www.cassiejwilliams.info
Email: cassiewilliams1818@gmail.com

Social Media:

Facebook: facebook.com/cassie.j.williams.3

Instagram: @cassietheencourager

LinkedIn: in/cassie-jones-williams-1a402522

Author Link: amazon.com/author/cassiejwilliams

Ways We Can Walk Together:

- Book me for your next conference, women's gathering, Bible study, or a church event
- Follow me on my socials for encouragement, updates, and free resources
- Schedule a one-on-one life coaching session
- Partner with us to help women rise from brokenness to boldness

Leave a Review:

If this book encouraged you, please consider leaving a review on Amazon or Goodreads. Your words could be exactly what someone else needs to find their way to something better. Amazon Link: https://a.co/d/8Ev2FtK

Let's continue this journey together.

Your best is yet to come.

— Dr. Cassie J. Williams

Also By This Author

Brave Enough to Pray: A Prayer Journal for Women

Confidence: Completing the Good Work in You

I Can't Lie to Myself, I Love Me: Self-Care Journal

The Christmas Tree Crumbs (Children's Book)

¿Por Qué No Perdonar?: Un plan de acción para la paz y la libertad (Spanish Edition)

What I Miss: A Journal to Help Teenagers Cope with Grief

When Tomorrow Starts Without You: A Grief Journal for Adults

Why Not Forgive: An Action Plan to Peace and Freedom

Article writings cited in Spring, Summer, Fall, and Winter Editions of Our Story Magazine.

Author Page: www.amazon.author/cassiejwilliams

Scripture References

Ecclesiastes 9:10 (NIV)
"Whatever your hand finds to do, do it with all your might..."

Ecclesiastes 9:16 (NIV)
"So I said, 'Wisdom is better than strength.' But the poor man's wisdom is despised, and his words are no longer heeded."

Genesis 1:28 (NKJV)
"Then God blessed them, and God said to them, 'Be fruitful and multiply; fill the earth and subdue it; have dominion over the fish of the sea, over the birds of the air, and over every living thing that moves on the earth.'"

Hebrews 11:40 (NIV)
"Since God had planned something better for us so that only together with us would they be made perfect."

Isaiah 43:19 (NIV)
"See, I am doing a new thing! Now it springs up; do you not perceive it? I am making a way in the wilderness and streams in the wasteland."

Jeremiah 30:20–22 (NLT)
"Their children will prosper as they did long ago. I will establish them as a nation before me, and I will punish anyone who hurts them... You will be my people, and I will be your God."

Luke 12:7 (NIV)
"Indeed, the very hairs of your head are all numbered. Don't be afraid; you are worth more than many sparrows."

Proverbs 18:21 (ESV)
"Death and life are in the power of the tongue, and those who love it will eat its fruits."

Proverbs 19:21 (NIV)
"Many are the plans in a person's heart, but it is the Lord's purpose that prevails."

Proverbs 23:7 (NKJV)
"For as he thinks in his heart, so is he."

Romans 8:28 (NLT)
"And we know that God causes everything to work together for the good of those who love God and are called according to his purpose for them."

Bible Translation Acknowledgments

References

Answers.com. "How Much Money Did Solomon Have?" Accessed June 1, 2024. http://www.answers.com/Q/How_much_money_did_Solomon_have

Children Learn What They Live. Accessed January 5, 2025. https://childrenlearnwhattheylive.com/

Cleveland Clinic. "Effects of Working Too Much." Accessed July 3, 2024. https://health.clevelandclinic.org/effects-of-working-too-much

Covey, Stephen R. "Sacrifice Really Means Giving Up Something Good for Something Better." Accessed January 5, 2025. https://quotefancy.com/quote/909525/Stephen-R-Covey-Sacrifice-really-means-giving-up-something-good-for-something-better

Ferrucci, Pierro. *The Power of Kindness.* New York: Tarcher Perigee, 2007.

Financial Planning Association. "The Psychology of Wealth: Psychological Factors Associated with High Income." Accessed July 15, 2024.

https://www.onefpa.org/journal/Pages/DEC14-The-Psychology-of-Wealth-Psychological-Factors-Associated-with-High-Income.aspx

Greenbook. "The 33% Rule: Learning from the Past and Embracing the Future." Accessed July 15, 2024. https://www.greenbook.org/insights/brand-strategy/the-33-rule-learning-from-the-past-and-embracing-the-future

Guyana Chronicle. "Planet Earth is Like a Mother Whose Children Have Lost All Sense of Direction and All Value in Life." Accessed June 1, 2024. https://guyanachronicle.com/2022/02/20/planet-earth-is-like-a-mother-whose-children-have-lost-all-sense-of-direction-and-all-value-in-life/

Help Guide. "Benefits of Play for Adults." Accessed July 3, 2024. https://www.helpguide.org/mental-health/wellbeing/benefits-of-play-for-adults

Merriam-Webster Dictionary. "Optimistic." Accessed July 3, 2024. https://www.merriam-webster.com/dictionary/optimistic

Munroe, Myles. *In Pursuit of Purpose.* New Kensington: Whitaker House, 1992.

The Preacher Diary. "The Wisdom of the Poor." Accessed July 15, 2024. https://thepreacherdiary.com/the-wisdom-of-the-poor

Warren, Rick. *The Purpose Driven Life.* Grand Rapids: Zondervan, 2002.

www.ingramcontent.com/pod-product-compliance
Lightning Source LLC
LaVergne TN
LVHW010932110826
845149LV00013B/2554

* 9 7 9 8 9 9 8 5 1 8 5 2 2 *